MADE IN
INDIA

by Satinder Kaur Chohan

‖SAMUEL FRENCH‖

FOR PRODUCTION ENQUIRIES

UNITED KINGDOM AND WORLD
EXCLUDING NORTH AMERICA
licensing@concordtheatricals.co.uk

020-7054-7298

NORTH AMERICA
info@concordtheatricals.com
1-866-979-0447

Each title is subject to availability from Concord Theatricals, depending upon country of performance.

---

photocopying, recording, videotaping, or otherwise, without the prior written permission of the publisher. No one shall share this title, or part of this title, to any social media or file hosting websites.

The moral right of Satinder Kaur Chohan to be identified as author of this work has been asserted in accordance with Section 77 of the Copyright, Designs and Patents Act 1988.

USE OF COPYRIGHTED MUSIC

A licence issued by Concord Theatricals to perform this play does not include permission to use the incidental music specified in this publication. In the United Kingdom: Where the place of performance is already licensed by the PERFORMING RIGHT SOCIETY (PRS) a return of the music used must be made to them. If the place of performance is not so licensed then application should be made to PRS for Music (www.prsformusic.com). A separate and additional licence from PHONOGRAPHIC PERFORMANCE LTD (www.ppluk.com) may be needed whenever commercial recordings are used. Outside the United Kingdom: Please contact the appropriate music licensing authority in your territory for the rights to any incidental music.

USE OF COPYRIGHTED THIRD-PARTY MATERIALS

Licensees are solely responsible for obtaining formal written permission from copyright owners to use copyrighted third-party materials (e.g., artworks, logos) in the performance of this play and are strongly cautioned to do so. If no such permission is obtained by the licensee, then the licensee must use only original materials that the licensee owns and controls. Licensees are solely responsible and liable for clearances of all third-party copyrighted materials, and shall indemnify the copyright owners of the play(s) and their licensing agent, Concord Theatricals Ltd., against any costs, expenses, losses and liabilities arising from the use of such copyrighted third-party materials by licensees.

IMPORTANT BILLING AND CREDIT REQUIREMENTS

If you have obtained performance rights to this title, please refer to your licensing agreement for important billing and credit requirements.

AUTHOR'S NOTE

Made in India was first developed as part of OffWestEnd.com's
Adopt A Playwright Award, which I received in 2013. Working
with my Adopted Playwright mentor/dramaturg Fin Kennedy,
I continued writing the play after its commission by Tamasha
Theatre Company, where Fin later became Artistic Director.

I first settled on the idea after reading a shocking article in
which a middle-class English woman described an Indian
village surrogate as her "vessel". With my Indian village roots,
the surrogate could have been any of my Indian female relatives
or if my parents had not emigrated to the UK, even me. The
story of those two women was loaded with so much conflicting
culture, emotion and politics, I knew I had to write a play
around that complex situation, to understand its fertile terrain.

When I began writing the play, commercial surrogacy was
rife in many countries. In the "surrogacy hub" of India, it
flourished as an unregulated multi-billion rupee industry, with
thousands of surrogacies a year. During the writing process,
Thailand, Nepal, Cambodia, Mexico – and India – introduced
varying commercial surrogacy bans. The proposed ban in India
upended much of my original story. Yet it captured a global
trend in which legislation began reeling in the rapid advance of
science, especially that of Assisted Reproductive Technologies
(ART) and the creation of "non-traditional" family forms. From
being staunchly anti-commercial surrogacy, I realised the ban
highlighted more than a black and white situation, especially
for the impoverished women who had scant options to make as
much money elsewhere.

Made in India is about gender, economics, reproductive
technology and ethics. Globally and locally, we live in a
market society where "everything is for sale" including health,
education, emotions and bodies. Too often, morals are sacrificed
for rampant financial markets. Western consumers rely on
low-cost, low-paid global workers to provide the material
stuff of their lives, in the cheapest, most efficient, fastest ways
possible – whether a pair of trainers, or a baby. In that power

dynamic, consumers can afford to ignore marginalised workers in other parts of the world, their lives and struggles, rather than understand how we connect to them.

Commercial surrogacy felt like a fitting metaphor for it all. These (substitute Western) workers labour for profit-driven businesses and affluent global clients whether in the garment, electronics or other sweatshop industries – exploitation or empowerment, oppression or opportunity, there is still much to do to protect them. Profit is valued over workers and human dignity is sacrificed for a quick blood-stained buck. *Made in India* seeks to show how our material choices and demands shape our inequitable world.

For Tamasha's production, director Katie Posner created this world using minimal props. In pre-rehearsal drafts, I had centred the play around a (medical/dorm) bed. Katie boldly jettisoned the bed, rendering the world of the play a more fluid space. The stripped-down clinic became slightly out of time, in a sort of womb hyperreality. Lydia Denno's stunning set of cyclical and moveable fabric medical screens, made of timber-framed threaded "looms", connected the garment and surrogacy industries. The screens moved around on a central playing circle of off-white clinical tiles, bordered by a deep red Indian fabric printed floor, bleeding in. By creating this fragile womb-like interior, the set inextricably bound these three women, their bodies and emotions to each other.

The script is open to creative interpretation and a big imagination – not least in the transitions. Projections on the screens, voiceovers and music in the clinic space create both individual and collective consciousness. Prema Mehta's lighting, Shanaz Gulzar's AV designs and Arun Ghosh's soundscape beautifully textured Tamasha's production. Yet the transitions can be done simply and selectively, enough to suggest inner worlds and a bigger world outside, whilst keeping a narrative flow.

For the Gujarati spoken by both Dr. Gupta and Aditi (in scenes involving only the two of them), a couple of lines of Gujarati can establish their mother tongue and then be followed by lines in English (to denote fluent Gujarati).

Like Tamasha's production, any staging of *Made in India* can be done impressionistically. Placing these three female lives, their stories, bodies and emotions centre stage, enables us to see all that commercial surrogacy and its biological, financial and emotional transactions entail – in all its messy complexity.

Satinder Kaur Chohan
2017

With very special thanks to:

Sofie Mason
Diana Jervis-Read
Declan Feenan

All Angels for the Adopt A Playwright Award 2013-2014

All at the Centre for Family Research at the University of
Cambridge, especially Susan Golombok, Vasanti Jadva and
Nishtha Lamba

Chris White
Chetna Pandya
Sheena Bhattessa
Kate Hooper
Olivia Poulet
Sofia Stuart
Kirsty Bushell
Pooja Ghai
Sudha Buchar
Susie Trayling
Krupa Pattani
Charlotte Randle
Peter Singh

For their role in the development of *Made in India*

Made in India was first performed on 24th January 2017 at the Belgrade Theatre, Coventry. It opened at Soho Theatre, London on 8th March 2017 with the following cast:

CAST

Eva   Gina Isaac
Dr Gupta   Syreeta Kumar
Aditi   Ulrika Krishnamurti

CREATIVE TEAM

Written by   Satinder Kaur Chohan
Directed by   Katie Posner
Dramaturg   Fin Kennedy
Designer   Lydia Denno
Composer and Sound Designer   Arun Ghosh
Lighting Designer   Prema Mehta
AV Designer   Shanaz Gulzar
Casting Director   Nadine Rennie
Assistant Director   Corey Campbell
(supported by the Regional Theatre Young Directors Scheme)
Assistant Lighting Designer   Rachel Cleary
(supported by the Association of Lighting Designers Lumière Scheme)

PRODUCTION TEAM

Production Manager   Dennis Charles
Company Stage Manager   Laura Stevens
Technical Stage Manager   Emma Atherton
Press Consultant   Nancy Poole PR
Publicity Photography   Sophia Schorr-Kon
Rehearsal Photography   Katherine Leedale
Promotional Video   Fionn Robson Guilfoyle
Production Photography   Robert Day

CHARACTERS

DR. GUPTA – Indian fertility clinic owner,
in her late 30s/early 40s

EVA – English client, in her late 30s/early 40s

ADITI – Indian rural village woman, 28

TRIMESTER ONE

Scene One

Indian spring.

Lajja Gauri Fertility Clinic, Gujarat, India.

Meeting room.

Street sounds cascade into a near-empty room. Political slogans and "Bharat Mata Ki Jai" ('Victory to Mother India') chants punch the air. Cars and rickshaws honk. Bullock carts roll. Cowbells jangle. Passing street vendors yell and shout, selling their wares. Bright white sunlight pushes through an iron-barred window. White paint on the walls bubbles and blisters in the heat. Posters of white mothers and babies, the Virgin Mary with baby Jesus, Krishna and Goddess Lajja Gauri cover peeling patches. A ceiling fan whirs above scattered plastic chairs. Dressed in light linen, EVA *wheels in a travel case, drops her bag and fans herself with a file, scanning the room. In a white medical coat over a bright sari and chappals,* DR. GUPTA *strides in, hanging up her smartphone.*

DR. GUPTA *(holding out her hand)* Welcome to India Mrs. Roe –

EVA *(shaking* DR. GUPTA*'s hand)* Eva, please.

DR. GUPTA *pulls a scrunched garland from a pocket, hanging it around* EVA*'s neck.*

DR. GUPTA – and welcome to my world-famous Lajja Gauri Clinic!

EVA *(admiring the garland)* Marigolds? So colourful. Thank you.

DR. GUPTA Actually, I didn't expect you till tomorrow.

EVA *(holding up a newspaper)* Dr. Gupta, I read about a possible surrogacy ban –

DR. GUPTA Please, don't worry.

EVA – in the car, from the airport.

DR. GUPTA Flares up now and again like an irritating rash –

EVA But it says –

DR. GUPTA – then dies down.

EVA The Government isn't introducing a ban?

DR. GUPTA Too much to lose.

EVA I've nothing to worry about?

DR. GUPTA Not so close to a state election. Thakkar has assured me.

EVA If we need to start sooner –

DR. GUPTA He's a leading election candidate. If anything changes, I'll let you know. Immediately.

EVA You're sure?

DR. GUPTA I'm sure.

EVA Ok, thank you.

EVA *puts away the newspaper.*

DR. GUPTA Mrs. Roe, I'm so honoured you chose my clinic.

EVA I'm relieved to be here – finally.

DR. GUPTA You've been so brave, fighting the British courts. Your landmark case proved how anachronistic laws fail to keep pace with science.

EVA Not without financial cost, blinding media glare, vitriolic abuse –

DR. GUPTA "Mrs. R" made seismic waves and won.

EVA Now "Mrs. R's" real work can begin.

DR. GUPTA *(pointing at the picture)* Goddess Lajja Gauri will look over you.

EVA *(admiring the picture)* She's a powerful brand image.

DR. GUPTA You think?

EVA With those breasts and that vulva? I work in advertising.

DR. GUPTA I'm expanding my clinic. We're re-launching soon. I'd love to get your advice.

EVA I'd be happy to help.

DR. GUPTA Great! Let's carve out time later. *(Ushering out EVA)* For now, don't fret, get rest, tomorrow is for you. Today is for your surrogate.

EVA *(not moving)* That's also why I'm here.

DR. GUPTA You don't need to be.

EVA You didn't receive my email?

DR. GUPTA About –?

EVA I'd like to choose my surrogate.

Pause.

DR. GUPTA Eva, leave final selection to me.

EVA You're scheduled to choose today anyway –

DR. GUPTA Meet her down the line –

EVA I rushed straight here –

DR. GUPTA – when we confirm a pregnancy –

EVA I'm here.

DR. GUPTA – when we sign a contract. Much better time for you both.

EVA I'm here.

DR. GUPTA *slides the travel case back to* EVA.

DR. GUPTA You've had a long journey. Why don't you head to the hotel?

EVA I'd like to / begin here –

DR. GUPTA Check in, unpack / relax –

EVA – crash at the hotel later.

DR. GUPTA West-East is more taxing than East-West. You must be jetlagged.

EVA I'm on Indian time.

DR. GUPTA When you're a day early? A day late, maybe!

EVA In London, I've been waking, eating, sleeping five and a half hours earlier –

DR. GUPTA You're joking?

EVA To be ready.

DR. GUPTA You've got a demanding few days ahead –

EVA I'm ready.

DR. GUPTA Don't underestimate how much rest you need –

EVA I haven't.

DR. GUPTA It's not all about the surrogate. It's about the real mother too.

EVA I'll leave as soon as we've chosen her.

Pause.

DR. GUPTA Eva –

EVA I want to ensure she's a good fit.

DR. GUPTA Every one of our 100 surrogates-to-be is an excellent fit.

EVA *(holding out the file)* The clinic emailed me profiles a few days ago.

DR. GUPTA Reference only.

EVA *(flicks through the file)* I'd like to meet... *(Holds up a page)* Surrogate 32.

DR. GUPTA This isn't egg donor selection.

EVA I'd like to meet *her.*

DR. GUPTA There won't be any genetic link between *her* and your baby –

EVA I know.

DR. GUPTA I'll select the healthiest uterus available. Endometrial lining inch perfect for your embryo. We've several surrogates good to go.

EVA Surrogate 32.

DR. GUPTA Surrogate 43 is prime, at the ready –

EVA *(pointing to a photo)* Is Surrogate 32 here, at the clinic?

DR. GUPTA Why her?

> EVA *stares at the photo.*

> Eva, medical conditions need to be optimum. I select the surrogate who best fits your cycle when we begin, so both your bodies fall quickly into sync.

EVA This shouldn't be a blind date.

DR. GUPTA We'll arrange a meeting once embryo transfer succeeds.

EVA I want to meet my surrogate before I begin. She'll give birth to my baby.

DR. GUPTA It's not clinic procedure for you to meet so soon.

EVA I'm a paying client.

DR. GUPTA Other paying clients don't want to meet their surrogates this early, if at all.

EVA I do.

> *Pause.*

DR. GUPTA Please, have a seat.

EVA I'm fine standing.

DR. GUPTA We only discourage contact at this stage to protect you and the surrogate. If you meet now, it sets you both up for disappointment if the transfer fails. Meet her when we confirm a pregnancy. A meeting isn't necessary now.

EVA What is necessary?

DR. GUPTA You supply your eggs. Your husband, his sperm.

EVA The cryo-shipment is still here at the clinic?

DR. GUPTA Yes, it's safe with us.

Pause.

EVA *(teary)* Eleven years of failed IVF cycles. Not knowing if I'd ever get pregnant. Getting pregnant, trying to stay pregnant – three times. "No heartbeat" – three times. Then... Tom...the courts...work I need to pay for *(stops herself)* –

DR. GUPTA *hands* **EVA** *a tissue.*

I'm alone...out of time...

Pause. **EVA** *wipes her tears.*

DR. GUPTA The surrogate is only the carrier. You're "renting"her womb.

EVA "Renting?"

DR. GUPTA This is a transaction.

EVA For your other clients, maybe.

DR. GUPTA Best you see it that way too.

EVA Please, bring her in.

DR. GUPTA Eva –

EVA Please. Please.

DR. GUPTA *pauses, then exits.* EVA *removes the garland and drinks dry her bottled water. She paces around, slapping mosquitoes on her naked skin. The door sounds.* EVA *wipes her face, smoothes her hair.* ADITI *shuffles in behind* DR. GUPTA, *head bowed, barefoot, adjusting the hanging pallu of her best sari over her face and bun. She wears gold earrings, a nose stud and mehndi on her hands. She carries a scrunched plastic bag.* DR. GUPTA *lowers the pallu, revealing* ADITI's *face.* EVA *is transfixed by* ADITI, *who keeps her head bowed.*

DR. GUPTA *(presenting* ADITI*)* Surrogate 32.

EVA *(to* ADITI*)* Hello. What's your name?

DR. GUPTA Ah-dithi. Or call her Ada. Or Addy. Or Adith. Like Adith Piaf!

EVA A-ditty?

DR. GUPTA *nods in encouragement.* EVA *offers her hand to* ADITI.

Hello, I'm Eva.

Confused, ADITI *turns to* DR. GUPTA.

DR. GUPTA *(to* ADITI*)* "Madamji".

ADITI *(pressing her hands together for* EVA*)* Namaste Madamji.

EVA *(quickly presses her hands together)* No – ma – stay.

DR. GUPTA *moves to get a chair for* ADITI.

Thank you Doctor. I can take over now –

DR. GUPTA – and communicate how?

EVA She doesn't speak English?

DR. GUPTA Not yet.

EVA Any English?

DR. GUPTA She will soon. I run daily intensive English classes for all my surrogates. Plus computer, internet, sewing, knitting, yoga, hair and make-up classes, all in the dorm upstairs. I even set up bank accounts in their names. Surrogacy isn't just for one baby or five. It's to set up these women for life. *(To* **ADITI***)* Bhaito.

EVA You really take care of them.

DR. GUPTA We spoil our surrogates 24/7 for nine months.

As she sits, **ADITI** *drops her bag.* **EVA** *hands the bag to* **ADITI***, who clutches it without looking at* **EVA***.* **EVA** *sits opposite* **ADITI***, taking a sheet from her file.* **DR. GUPTA** *takes the bag from* **ADITI***, placing it under* **ADITI**'s *chair.*

EVA *(holding up the sheet)* Just a few questions –

DR. GUPTA I have to get to a meeting, so...

EVA Aditi, how old are you?

DR. GUPTA That information is in the profile.

EVA Can I hear the answers from Aditi?

DR. GUPTA This is a busy clinic –

EVA I don't want to waste time.

DR. GUPTA *(to* **ADITI** *in Gujarati)* Age?

ADITI *(in Gujarati)* 28.

DR. GUPTA *(to* **EVA***)* 28.

EVA *(to* **ADITI***)* Pregnancy sweet spot *and* light years younger than me!

EVA *looks to* **DR. GUPTA** *to translate.* **DR. GUPTA** *does not translate.*

(To **ADITI***)* Are you married? If you are, what does your husband think about the surrogacy? Did he or anyone else pressure you to do this?

DR. GUPTA Again, have you read her profile?

EVA Can you ask Aditi?

DR. GUPTA "Ah-dithi".

EVA So it's not just dry data.

DR. GUPTA Or "Ada" if that's too difficult.

EVA *(repeats)* Ah – ditty. Ah – ditty. Ah –

> **ADITI** *looks up at* **EVA**. **EVA** *smiles at her.*

DR. GUPTA *(to* **ADITI** *in Gujarati)* Married?

ADITI *(in Gujarati)* My husband was a fruit and veg seller. Crushed under his cart by a rich drunk in a big speeding car. Bhagwan *(points upwards)* looks after him now.

DR. GUPTA Husband is dead.

EVA She's a widow? *(Holding up the profile.)* This says "*Not married*"...

DR. GUPTA Breadwinner of her family now.

EVA Aditi, what happened to your –?

DR. GUPTA Not fruitful to visit the past.

EVA Please tell her I'm so sorry about her husband.

DR. GUPTA *(to* **ADITI** *in Gujarati)* She offers condolences.

> **ADITI** *lifts her eyes to meet* **EVA**'s, *nodding her head in thanks.*

EVA Aditi, how many children do you have?

DR. GUPTA Two daughters.

EVA Can you ask Aditi please?

DR. GUPTA *(to* **ADITI** *in Gujarati)* How many children?

ADITI *(in Gujarati)* Two girls. Both very hard-working at school, home, in the fields. Madamji, the eldest wants to be a doctor like you, helping the helpless. The youngest wants a cell phone and to work in a call-centre. She likes to talk. I'll buy them an education with this money. A future. Then they can be whoever they want to be.

DR. GUPTA Two daughters.

EVA That's all?

DR. GUPTA That's all. Two daughters. No sons.

ADITI *(to DR. GUPTA in Gujarati)* Madamji, my answers are ok?

EVA She has a question?

DR. GUPTA No questions. Just wants to know your next one.

EVA *(to ADITI)* Did you go to school?

DR. GUPTA *(to ADITI in Gujarati)* You didn't go to school...?

ADITI *(shaking her head, then in Gujarati)* Not for long. I had to stop to work in the fields with my mother. I'm a daughter of the soil.

DR. GUPTA High school graduate.

EVA But she shook her head / to say no –

DR. GUPTA She'd have gone to university / if her family could have afforded it. Thanks to you, she'll be able to send both her daughters to university.

EVA *(smiling at ADITI)* I really hope so.

DR. GUPTA Next question?

EVA Aditi, you live close to the clinic?

DR. GUPTA *(to ADITI in Gujarati)* You live where?

ADITI *(in Gujarati)* Padri. Two hours by bus. We live in a mud hut, with a leaky roof, where the rain runs in. I'd like to fix it or buy a new brick house –

DR. GUPTA *(interrupts)* Small village. Short bus journey away.

EVA If you move to the dorm here, will someone look after your daughters?

DR. GUPTA *(to* ADITI *in Gujarati)* When you move here, who will care for your daughters?

ADITI *(in Gujarati)* Their grandmother, in her village. Not my mother, my husband's mother. My mother is furious that I –

DR. GUPTA *(interrupts)* Paternal grandma in her village.

EVA *(to* ADITI*)* Your children won't be far?

DR. GUPTA So close, they can visit on designated family days. Occasionally.

EVA *(to* DR. GUPTA*)* That's reassuring. Aditi, do you work?

DR. GUPTA *(to* ADITI *in Gujarati)* Occupation?

ADITI *(in Gujarati)* I milk cows, do chores on a dairy farm – when I get work.

DR. GUPTA Dairy farm labourer. Gujarat might be a dry state for alcohol –

EVA This is a dry state?

DR. GUPTA – but thanks to our famous White Revolution, it's a fertile state for milk. Milk *and* surrogate capital of India!

EVA No booze?

DR. GUPTA Bootleg always available. For a small fee.

EVA Thank God.

DR. GUPTA Eva, Gujarat has made much of its vast wealth from milk. Aditi is one of the women who makes the milk flow here. And you'll make the money flow for her. In nine months as your surrogate, she'll earn what it would take her ten years to earn as a labourer.

EVA I'll make that much of a difference?

DR. GUPTA Life-changing. You'll lift her and her daughters out of extreme poverty, give them opportunities – university, jobs – they'd never have. *You.* Now *(moving towards the door)* –

EVA Just a couple more questions –

DR. GUPTA *(speeding up* EVA*)* My meeting?

EVA *(to* ADITI*)* Any problems with previous pregnancies? Miscarriages? Personal or family health issues?

DR. GUPTA Clean sheet.

EVA If you could...

DR. GUPTA *(to* ADITI *in Gujarati)* Any problems giving birth?

ADITI *(smiling, in Gujarati)* Both daughters slipped out like butter.

EVA *(smiling)* What did she say?

DR. GUPTA This virgin surrogate says she'll deliver a healthy bouncing baby for you. Strong uterus like that, she's got more surrogacies in her yet! Ok, you've more than enough information and should really rest –

EVA Can I have time with Aditi? Alone?

DR. GUPTA And communicate how?

EVA *(holding up her phone)* Google Translate?

DR. GUPTA She's answered all your questions.

EVA Only a few minutes.

DR. GUPTA My meeting.

EVA I'll pay her, for her time.

DR. GUPTA *(to* ADITI *in Gujarati)* Bhagwan, she's a fussy one... Smile. A lot. *(Exiting, to* EVA*)* Five minutes.

ADITI *(calling after* DR. GUPTA*)* Madamji? Madamji?

> ADITI *grabs her bag and scuttles after* DR. GUPTA, *who slams the door shut.* ADITI *faces the closed door, turns slowly and sits back down, avoiding eye contact with* EVA, *who taps into her phone.* ADITI *clutches her bag close.*

EVA Typical. *(Stops tapping)* No reception.

EVA *puts away her phone. Silence.* EVA *smiles at* ADITI. ADITI *averts her gaze.*

Aditi? You chose to be a surrogate? Why?

ADITI *stares at the floor.*

Money, yes. But why else? You, a surrogate –

EVA *repeats actions of a protruding stomach.*

– why?

ADITI *raises her head slightly, eyes downcast.*

Are you happy to do this *(patting her stomach)*?

ADITI *lowers her head again.*

Ready, to do this *(patting her stomach)*?

EVA *crouches in front of* ADITI.

Aditi, look at me.

ADITI *lowers her head.*

Look at me.

ADITI *fiddles with her bag.*

Is this how you'll bring my baby into the world? Without looking at me?

ADITI *interlaces her fingers and bows her head.*

"Blessed art thou amongst women and blessed is the fruit of thy womb". *(Pause)* Look me in the eye. I won't hurt you. Not after everything you've been through. Everything I've been through. Everything lost.

Pause. ADITI *levels eyes at* EVA. *Lights out. A magic lantern projection of syringes, overflowing with blood, circles the clinic walls to the music of a Catholic hymn. The music underscores an election rally speech "With our technological tools, let's plant miracle seeds of the future, in the fertile soil of our dreams. To make a New India that grows and prospers. An India reborn."*

Scene Two

Procedure room.

A loud ringing phone. EVA *answers, half-way through undressing and slipping on a medical gown, as* DR. GUPTA *waits, an open medical file in her hand.*

EVA Hi Mike, how are you? No, not a problem to speak. No, it's not interfering. I'm meeting him in Mumbai next week. Yes, I'll send that on. Ok great. Thanks Mike. *(Hangs up)*

EVA *resumes putting on her medical gown, back to front. An IV is inserted into her hand.* DR. GUPTA *resumes reading from the file.*

DR. GUPTA You've completed thirteen days of hormonal treatment. You were away for most of it?

EVA About ten days. I travelled to –

DR. GUPTA – kept up with all your fertility shots?

EVA Injected between the nausea, lassi cravings –

DR. GUPTA Had your final trigger shot at midnight?

EVA Has hard-boiling eggs ever been more painful?

DR. GUPTA You and Aditi are cycling in sync. Her uterus is ripening perfectly.

EVA*'s phone rings.*

EVA *(glancing at her phone)* Great. I'll be here for any embryo transfer –

DR. GUPTA We can discuss any transfer by phone, should fertilisation work.

EVA I'd like to be with Aditi if it happens –

DR. GUPTA You don't need to be.

EVA But I –

The phone stops ringing. EVA *glances at her phone.*

DR. GUPTA Eva, focus on your job first.

> DR. GUPTA *snaps on a pair of latex gloves and reaches towards* EVA.

Relax. It's all very straightforward –

EVA *(stopping* DR. GUPTA*)* Blood...blood...on your gloves.

DR. GUPTA *(checking her gloves)* A mere spot. Easily dispensed with.

> DR. GUPTA *throws away the gloves and reaches for a new pair.*

EVA *(pointing)* Blood...blood...on the box.

> DR. GUPTA *wipes the box with a tissue and throws it away. She snaps on the new pair of gloves.*

DR. GUPTA Nurse will be reprimanded. It won't happen again.

EVA Do you change the sheets every time?

DR. GUPTA Lie down. Please.

> EVA *hugs herself.*

Lose more time, we'll have to delay your treatment, begin again, midnight trigger shot and all –

EVA You're going inside me, with surgical instruments, to extract my eggs –

DR. GUPTA I've done this procedure thousands of times –

EVA What if your equipment is dirty?

DR. GUPTA Our equipment is / state of the art, clean –

EVA I get infected?

DR. GUPTA You've never seen stray blood in a UK clinic?

EVA Not when I'm paying thousands for my treatment, no.

DR. GUPTA Then don't let it affect you. You won't see it again.

EVA Outside, I can deal with the dirt, the stench, sewage, defecation – but this isn't the Indian roadside. If you're taking out the few eggs I've got left, this should be a spotless, sterile clinic.

Pause.

DR. GUPTA *(taking off her gloves)* Ok, let's cancel.

The phone rings again. EVA *is caught between* DR. GUPTA *and her ringing phone.*

EVA What?

DR. GUPTA I'm cancelling. Good luck finding what you need out there.

EVA Dr. Gupta –

DR. GUPTA *hands* EVA *her belongings and her ringing phone.*

You can't.

DR. GUPTA Mrs. Roe, you arrived a day early, unannounced.

EVA I was worried about the ban / wanted to meet –

DR. GUPTA Breaching clinic policy, I let you select your surrogate on the spot –

EVA I'm so grateful –

DR. GUPTA I also allowed you to use your dead husband's sperm –

EVA – you've been incredibly compassionate –

DR. GUPTA – when most clinics in India, in fact, the world, would not –

EVA – and understanding.

DR. GUPTA You're delaying your treatment. My other clients' too. My clinic adheres to global standards but if you think it's dirty, unhygienic –

EVA No, no, I don't, not at all –

DR. GUPTA – take your business elsewhere. I can pick and choose my business. As you can. Don't like my service? Find a cleaner, cheaper, more flexible option elsewhere. That's the real beauty of New India.

The phone stops ringing.

EVA *(joins her hands together)* Please, forgive me. This is the right clinic. You're the right doctor. You've done so much for me already. It's just...the hormone shots, bloated ovaries, bruised womb...always reaching for Tom but...he's never there...keeping order when I feel so messed up – I'm just – not thinking...because...all I'm thinking is...what if...what if... I don't have...any eggs left? Any eggs at all?

Long pause.

DR. GUPTA We'll only know when we try.

DR. GUPTA *places* **EVA**'s *belongings back to one side. She reopens the file.*

On your ultrasound, you have seven mature follicles – five more than when you began. A growth spurt. Must be a few eggs to be needled out.

EVA You're doing your job. Tom has done his. Aditi is ready to do hers. Only if I do mine will I be a real mother. A real woman.

EVA's *phone rings again.*

(Picking it up) I'll switch it – *(looking at the screen).*

DR. GUPTA Eva, your eggs are only fresh for a limited time.

EVA Not if work over boil them first.

DR. GUPTA I've several caesarians lined up after you. But if you'd rather –

EVA *puts away her phone.*

EVA Sorry. *(Deep breath)* Let's crack on with my Easter Egg hunt.

DR. GUPTA *(reading the file)* We should extract five or six eggs, at least –

EVA Only five or six?

DR. GUPTA Magic numbers for a woman over 40.

DR. GUPTA *jabs the IV line into* **EVA***'s hand.*

Only takes one golden egg to make a baby.

DR. GUPTA *flaps* **EVA***'s gown.*

But maybe put this on the right way first.

EVA *(looking at her gown)* Oh, I didn't...

DR. GUPTA *helps* **EVA** *with her gown, distracted by a tattoo on* **EVA***'s naked back.*

DR. GUPTA What is that?

EVA A Hindu good luck symbol. Henna. Fading already.

DR. GUPTA This? For good luck?

EVA Sweetest little girl clung to me till I got it.

DR. GUPTA You did it round here?

EVA The Ganges. Stayed in the same hotel from my honeymoon.

DR. GUPTA An Indian honeymoon?

EVA Tom backpacked around India before uni. Insisted we come here. He took me to Rajasthan, Goa, Kerala... But he loved the mad Ganges.

DR. GUPTA Ah, the murky brown water, burning flesh, naked sadhus –

EVA He loved it all... So I took him back there. On a long boat. Poured milk, floated flowers and candles, priest chanting, naked sadhus dancing, demonstrators shouting, emptied him into the flow. I did what I needed to do.

DR. GUPTA You will here too.

DR. GUPTA *hands* EVA *a hairnet, which she puts on.*

To reiterate, we enter with a very fine needle, insert it through the vaginal wall –

EVA Know it like a Catholic hymn.

DR. GUPTA When you come round next door, you'll see other clients recovering next to you –

EVA Other clients?

DR. GUPTA Once we've finished expanding, we'll have new procedure rooms, new birthing rooms, a new dormitory, a restaurant...

EVA Tom ran a restaurant. A small, organic one. He sold it, so we could have a baby.

EVA *makes the sign of the cross, as* DR. GUPTA *looks on.*

Lapsed Catholic. CEO. Christmas and Easter Only.

DR. GUPTA It's important to have faith.

EVA Even when it's been worn away?

DR. GUPTA Best time to find it. *(Pause)* Half hour. You won't feel a thing.

EVA The sheet...it's –

DR. GUPTA *stops.*

– clean.

DR. GUPTA Relax. Count down from ten to one for me...

DR. GUPTA *puts on her surgical mask.*

EVA Ten, nine, eight, seven, six...

Lights out. Hindu chants rise as magic lantern projections circle the clinic walls. Ashes and petals are poured from a clay pot into a fast-flowing river. The scattered ashes and petals on water dissolve into an egg and sperm making love and life in a petri dish. The egg and sperm fertilise. Embryos flower and grow.

Scene Three

Procedure room.

A voice on a background radio declares 'This ban is a grave disappointment. We believe surrogacy is a force for social good. Our great Bharat Mata nation, our Mother India, must not turn back now.'

Wiping tears, **ADITI** *paces around the room, as* **DR. GUPTA** *stands. A medical gown and hairnet are laid out close to* **ADITI**'s *plastic bag.* **DR. GUPTA** *and* **ADITI** *speak to each other in Gujarati. (The first line between them can be delivered in Gujarati and the rest in English, even if Gujarati is specified).*

ADITI *(in Gujarati)* Madamji, I've been waiting for you. *(Can be delivered in English from here)* How has this ended before we've begun?

DR. GUPTA It's a huge shock to us all.

ADITI All your strong pills, medicines, injections, my body ready to plant a seed.

DR. GUPTA You'll find something else.

ADITI Like what Madamji?

DR. GUPTA Back to the dairy farm?

ADITI When there's no work?

DR. GUPTA You're a clever woman.

ADITI How will I pay off all Manesh's and my loans? Our crippling debts?

DR. GUPTA Resourceful.

ADITI I didn't earn even a single rupee here.

DR. GUPTA No guarantee you would have got pregnant.

ADITI A chance.

DR. GUPTA We can't know now.

ADITI What about my daughters? My shack, full of holes?

DR. GUPTA We'll all suffer.

ADITI They want me to stay poor?

DR. GUPTA Those big people don't want you to get rich.

ADITI My only lifeline –

DR. GUPTA They should support us –

ADITI – out of the mud.

DR. GUPTA – not stop us.

ADITI Can't you do something?

DR. GUPTA I'm not one of the big people.

Pause.

ADITI You said the ban is for foreigners.

DR. GUPTA Too early to know what's going on.

ADITI Indians are still allowed?

DR. GUPTA It's unclear.

ADITI What do you know?

DR. GUPTA We think only married Indian couples are allowed. No foreigners. Close relatives as surrogates only. No payment involved.

ADITI What will I do?

DR. GUPTA I don't know what will happen.

ADITI You said you would protect me –

DR. GUPTA I have to tell the others now.

ADITI – look after me.

DR. GUPTA hands ADITI her bag, ushering her towards the door.

ADITI Madamji, I can cook, clean –

DR. GUPTA Aditi –

ADITI *(touching* DR. GUPTA*'s feet)* Be a maid –

DR. GUPTA I have to go.

    As DR. GUPTA *moves towards the door,* EVA *rushes in.*

EVA *(to* DR. GUPTA*)* You have / to do it.

DR. GUPTA Eva? /

ADITI Ewah?

EVA *(to* DR. GUPTA*)* You have to.

DR. GUPTA *(to* ADITI *in Gujarati)* You can go now.

    ADITI *reluctantly readies to leave, turning to* EVA.

EVA *(to* ADITI, *embracing her)* Stay.

DR. GUPTA *(to* EVA*)* I'd rather she –

EVA *(to* DR. GUPTA*)* This could be the last time I see her.

    DR. GUPTA *gestures to* ADITI *to stay.*

    (To DR. GUPTA*)* Please, you have / to do it –

DR. GUPTA A ban / is a ban.

EVA – for all of us.

DR. GUPTA Took effect at midnight –

EVA We're only a few hours over.

DR. GUPTA A crucial few hours over.

EVA I flew back from Mumbai immediately, cancelled my meeting.

DR. GUPTA I have to cancel a full day of transfers, other procedures, before cancelling weeks, months more. Over 100 couples –

EVA My embryos are ready to transfer *today*.

DR. GUPTA We're all in limbo.

EVA We're all here.

DR. GUPTA We think clients who have completed pre-ban transfers can continue. Those who have not, will not –

EVA We could do the transfer today.

DR. GUPTA Risk my job and reputation?

EVA My embryos are ready.

DR. GUPTA Risk my business?

EVA Aditi's right here –

DR. GUPTA Risk my whole clinic?

EVA We could tweak / papers, times, dates.

DR. GUPTA For one transfer?

EVA Pretend we did it yesterday.

DR. GUPTA I can't risk everything.

EVA I can't lose everything.

DR. GUPTA I didn't make the rules.

EVA But you can break them.

DR. GUPTA Not this one.

EVA I've got this far –

DR. GUPTA I know it's difficult.

EVA I can't stop now.

DR. GUPTA I'm sorry Eva.

Long pause.

EVA My embryos – what happens if we don't use them?

DR. GUPTA We have to keep them here –

EVA Unborn, frozen in time?

DR. GUPTA – by law.

EVA Till when?

DR. GUPTA Till something changes.

EVA Will it?

DR. GUPTA I don't know.

EVA I can't do a transfer and can't take my embryos – my unborn babies – with me when I leave?

DR. GUPTA Right now, no, you can't take them out of the country.

EVA This is my last chance.

DR. GUPTA We could appeal to the courts.

EVA Another legal battle?

DR. GUPTA Or start again, in another country.

EVA I've only enough left for here.

DR. GUPTA I'll help you find another clinic abroad.

EVA I've put everything into this.

DR. GUPTA I've poured myself into this too. Ploughed thousands and thousands of my own money into my clinic, the expansion, the – *(Stops herself)*

Pause.

EVA You assured me this wouldn't happen.

DR. GUPTA Caught us all unawares.

EVA I showed you the article –

DR. GUPTA If I had acted on every story, every rumour –

EVA We could have scheduled sooner.

DR. GUPTA You're not my only client.

Pause.

EVA Maybe I'm not meant to be a mother.

DR. GUPTA They're destroying all our dreams.

EVA Not meant to have our baby. His baby. My baby.

ADITI *(in English)* No baby Ewah?

EVA No baby.

> DR. GUPTA *moves to the door.* ADITI *takes out a crumpled photo from her bag, showing it to* EVA.

DR. GUPTA Aditi –

ADITI *(in English)* One. Two.

EVA Beautiful.

ADITI *(in English)* My.

EVA Look just like you.

ADITI *(in English)* Two girl. My.

EVA *(to* ADITI*)* Like their mum.

DR. GUPTA Once we know more, I'll be in touch. I'll let you know straight away if anything changes. Aditi come.

EVA I'll pay you extra for the transfer.

DR. GUPTA Enough to pay off all my debts – current and pending?

EVA I'll campaign with you against the ban, here and around the world if you need me. Use my contacts. Use my story.

DR. GUPTA I have so many stories Eva. I'm sorry.

EVA Did those women fight through the courts? Challenge "anachronistic" laws? Receive global press attention? I'm not done. Nor are you. "Eva Roe, the last foreign client in Dr. Gupta's clinic. Eva Roe's baby, the last foreign baby delivered by Dr. Gupta."

DR. GUPTA I'll do all I can to overturn the ban, within the law.

EVA At the same time, through the agency, I could help promote your clinic here and abroad.

DR. GUPTA I can't afford to hire your agency.

EVA We'll work pro-bono.

DR. GUPTA Pro-bono?

EVA We'll work on a Lajja Gauri brand and campaign – aimed at women like me who need to know your clinic exists. Take Lajja Gauri to countries where surrogacy is legal, use it to win arguments where it's illegal. Fight the ban and expand your brand.

DR. GUPTA Deep in debt, without investors?

EVA I'll put you in touch with any agency clients here – what about the state election? Thakkar?

DR. GUPTA If he's elected Chief Minister of Gujarat, he'll push to overturn the ban.

EVA Perfect! We'll need him.

Pause.

DR. GUPTA What if someone finds out about the transfer?

EVA Aditi and I don't bring complicated coupledom or a big family. No-one to tell if we keep it between us.

DR. GUPTA If you don't get pregnant?

EVA We tried. But – if we make it happen, we three women can hold up that baby – your clinic's last foreign surrogacy – and say we created a miracle life out of death. Together.

Pause.

DR. GUPTA You'll pay extra for the transfer?

EVA Whatever you think is a fair price.

DR. GUPTA Pay extra and work pro-bono?

EVA Whatever you need.

Long pause.

DR. GUPTA Eva, I – need you to get pregnant.

EVA Thank you.

> **DR. GUPTA** *and* **EVA** *shake hands.*

DR. GUPTA Aditi?

ADITI Madamji?

DR. GUPTA *(to* **ADITI** *in Gujarati)* You still ready to do this?

ADITI *(to* **DR. GUPTA** *in Gujarati)* Yes Madamji.

DR. GUPTA *(to* **ADITI** *in Gujarati)* Then listen to what I tell you.

ADITI *(to* **DR. GUPTA** *in Gujarati)* I'm listening.

> *In darkness,* **ADITI** *chants a Hindu mantra, growing louder, as an image swirls on the clinic walls, showing five embryos shoot into a womb. Two embryos attach themselves to the womb lining and grow. A baby's heartbeat rises from the chants, another baby's heartbeat emerges and overlaps, booming louder, as the image of a first ultrasound circles the walls.*

TRIMESTER TWO

Scene One

Roadside dhaba.

A dusty, humid haze hangs heavy. Sunlight slants into the dhaba, illuminating EVA *and* ADITI. *Street life, crackling oil and Bollywood sounds dance in the background. A couple of "Vote Thakkar" posters adorn the wall.* ADITI *is in a bright shalwar kameez with a chunni and yellow thread around her right wrist, her small baby bump protruding, while* EVA *wears a summery dress.* EVA *and* ADITI *drink lassis. A loud ringing phone.* EVA *answers.*

EVA *(on the phone)* Hi Mike, how are you? Yes all ok. No, not a problem to speak. No, it's not interfering. I'm really busy with meetings. Yes I understand but I always give a hundred percent. Yes, I'll send that on. Ok great. Thanks Mike. *(Hangs up)*

EVA gulps the last of her lassi and puts down her empty glass.

EVA Best lassi!

ADITI First time I go clinic, I smell this food on road, smell like Ma food *(Eyes closed, smells an imaginary gota, ready to bite)* One more...

EVA Nay!

ADITI Didi Ewah...please. Twin say, "Ma, one more gota"!

EVA Ma says, "No more deep-fried gotas!" *(Taking ADITI's hand)* Twins?

ADITI *(rubbing her stomach)* Twin smile you. Kiss you.

EVA My babies have grown, your English has grown –

ADITI Top Madamji class now!

EVA That's why *you* have to speak for all those surrogates.

ADITI Me try. All lady left in clinic, we hold Madamji paper. *(Holding a napkin above her head)* "Ban stop! Ban stop!"

EVA Yes, everyone must vote for Thakkar to stop the ban.

ADITI Madamji say Thakkar lose, we lose, so vote Thakkar every people! Me and Madamji put picture. All dhaba, all shop.

EVA You'll make people listen. But don't tire yourself out. Or the babies...

ADITI Only when you and Madamji say me.

EVA Before we start, I have something for you *(handing* ADITI *a small gift)*.

ADITI What is?

EVA To celebrate us getting pregnant.

> ADITI *unwraps the gift and lifts out a gold necklace with a lotus pendant.*

ADITI *(hugging* EVA*)* Thank you Ewah!

EVA *(hanging the necklace around* ADITI*'s neck)* Thank *you.*

ADITI *(admiring the pendant)* Kamala flower. All in my village.

EVA My husband wanted me to wear it if I ever got pregnant again.

ADITI Him no mind I wear?

EVA We're pregnant.

ADITI Ewah, where he is?

EVA Looks so pretty on you.

ADITI Me care this. Say him thank you.

> EVA *nods.*

EVA Right, let's do this, then get you back to the dorm.

ADITI *(patting her necklace)* Me ready!

EVA First – sit up straight, in front of the camera *(sitting up)*.

ADITI Back hurt.

EVA No slumping.

ADITI *(groaning, sitting up)* Oh Ewah, twin too fat, eat too much gota!

EVA Scarf over your head. *(Pulls the chunni over* **ADITI***'s head)* Respectable.

ADITI Eye down like Ma say me?

EVA Eyes straight at the interviewer when you talk.

> **ADITI** *laser focuses her eyes on* **EVA**.

> Aditi, why did you choose to be a surrogate?

ADITI Woman no baby, big shame. Big curse. People sorry you. Look you. Why wrong you? –

EVA *(interrupts)* Less how cursed I am, more how you're helping me...

ADITI I want give Didi Ewah baby. Make happy her. Same I happy two daughter.

EVA Great. What will you do with the money you earn as a surrogate?

ADITI Pay all rupee husband, me, take from bank, from village –

EVA No loans, debts. Good things, like the house, education...

ADITI I make brick house. No mud. Buy two daughter best school. Best life.

EVA Do you like being a surrogate?

ADITI Best job.

EVA With a smile, so we know you really mean it.

ADITI *(smiling a big fixed smile)* Best job.

EVA Aditi, what do you think about the ban on surrogacy?

ADITI Very bad. Why big people take job us? No help us? Care us? Them say "Make in India". So why we no make baby in India? We strong womans. You need, pay, we make. We womans make in India all thing, all time – clothe, house, road, baby –

EVA Yes!

ADITI I cut open tum tum for rupee. Now this bad people want me open leg for rupee? Open leg, feed daughter?

EVA Maybe don't mention cutting open tum tums, opening legs...

ADITI Why big people say my tum tum this do, no do? Them no feed me, so no say me what in tum tum put.

EVA Because it's your body, your choice to do what you want with it.

ADITI Haan. Why this people choose? I choose. My body, my choose.

EVA Perfect! Use that.

ADITI I this choose cos I no other choose.

EVA But you still chose to be a surrogate. You weren't forced into it –

ADITI But Ewah, I has no choose. Where I make so big rupee? Clinic only.

EVA No need to talk about that. "My body, my choice", says everything.

ADITI "My body, my choose".

EVA "Choice", like "voice".

ADITI "My voice, my choice".

EVA Exactly!

ADITI But family no like.

EVA Why?

ADITI Say I do bad thing with man.

EVA They don't understand Madamji's clever work.

ADITI Say me dirty.

EVA No. You're doing one of the most brave and beautiful things one woman can do for another woman.

ADITI Say Rajni, Rekha no see me with baby.

EVA Is that why they don't visit you?

ADITI I no tell village people. Ewah, them see me in TV? No want them see me.

EVA They'll be too busy watching those "dramas" you surrogates love, to see you on a news report, if we can get you on one.

ADITI Haan, village love dramas too much. Or I this do *(covers face with her chunni).*

EVA Keep answers to the ban, how wrong it is, how surrogacy is right for you, bad things that will happen after the ban –

ADITI *(uncovering her face)* What bad?

EVA The ban won't stop surrogacy. Secret clinics will continue doing it.

ADITI Give address me.

EVA Don't even think about it.

ADITI Why no?

EVA They're bad, dirty clinics that will push women like you into having babies, treat you badly, pay you badly, if they pay at all –

ADITI How they can?

EVA That's why we need / to stop the ban.

ADITI How no pay? This work no easy. Miss daughter. Pill, medicine, jection – so big sharp. Get sick, very sick –

EVA Morning sickness.

ADITI I hurt, cry –

EVA Aditi, I know –

   DR. GUPTA *rushes in.*

DR. GUPTA *(to* ADITI*)* There you are!

EVA *(to* DR. GUPTA*)* We were about to leave –

DR. GUPTA *(to* EVA*)* We were / searching –

EVA Just practising / questions –

DR. GUPTA – for her everywhere!

EVA Getting Aditi –

DR. GUPTA Frantic with worry!

EVA – media friendly.

DR. GUPTA We agreed to do that *on* the premises.

EVA We're not far.

DR. GUPTA One step outside my clinic without permission is far enough.

EVA It was a small treat.

DR. GUPTA Keeping them healthy and safe from the chaos out here, it's what you pay for.

EVA I'm sorry.

DR. GUPTA You're having twins. She needs double care.

EVA It won't happen again –

DR. GUPTA Ensure it doesn't.

EVA – especially as I'm back now till the birth.

DR. GUPTA Till...the birth?

EVA Great news. My bosses in London have given me more time to scout for Indian clients. No need to rush back! So I'm here to help, with the campaign, the twins – I won't get in the way.

DR. GUPTA I sent you a revised invoice for the embryo transfer.

EVA All I seem to do lately is pay off debts.

Pause.

DR. GUPTA *(spotting* **ADITI***'s necklace)* You went shopping too?

EVA No, that's a gift from me.

DR. GUPTA *(gesturing for the necklace, to* **ADITI** *in Gujarati)* Necklace.

ADITI *(to* **DR. GUPTA** *in Gujarati)* But Madamji –

ADITI begins taking off the necklace.

DR. GUPTA *(to* **EVA***)* Won't look good there. We don't want people thinking our surrogates are better off than they are.

EVA Where?

DR. GUPTA Aditi's about to address a big rally for Thakkar. He's agreed to take on the ban as one of his campaign highlights.

EVA That's fantastic news. Can I join?

DR. GUPTA He knows when we build up all our Aditis, we'll build up our Mother India. Then a superpower New India will truly be born.

ADITI hands the necklace to DR. GUPTA.

(To **EVA***)* No gifts between parents and surrogates.

EVA Of course.

DR. GUPTA Your payments will be enough. *(To* **ADITI***)* Challo.

On the clinic walls, a media montage of ADITI, DR. GUPTA and EVA at a rural election rally, dissolve into the monochrome image of a 12-week ultrasound scan. Two fully-formed foetuses float to the words of DR. GUPTA's rally speech "Don't hoard, or undervalue, or undersell our precious natural resources in the global bazaar. From our farmers feeding the world, our factories clothing the world, our IT workers connecting the world to our surrogates birthing the children of the world, sell the proud produce of India to the highest bidders and watch the wealth flow back for each of us. Money karma. Give out and we all get back". The rural crowd cheers.

Scene Two

The dorm.

Sunlight slices through an iron barred window, illuminating a picture of a crawling white baby and a "Vote Thakkar" poster on the pink wall. A television flickers, playing a rolling news channel on the election trail. ADITI *is dressed in a maternity dress, jasmine flowers in her hair and fresh make-up on her face. Her bump is bigger.* EVA *is wearing an Indian tunic with jeans, jasmine flowers in her hair and a chunni tied across her torso. Gujarati music plays loudly on* EVA's *phone.* ADITI *leads* EVA *with garba moves, circling a garba pot lit up by a diya. A half-sewn baby kurta lies close by.* ADITI *dances more slowly than* EVA. *Breathless,* ADITI *stops, distracted by the pot.*

EVA *(dancing)* Like this?

ADITI *(picking up the pot)* Rekha make same garba pot home.

EVA *(stops dancing)* I said to the owner, "Arrey bhai! Itna mahange kyon?"

ADITI *(laughing)* You say?

EVA 'Dena tai toh deh.'

ADITI *(laughing)* Ewah top Aditi class!

EVA Then he knocked off a few rupees.

ADITI *puts down the pot and sits, breathing fast, rubbing her stomach.*

(Holding out her hand) One more dance?

ADITI Too much Rekha, Rajni pull sari, "Ma, garba dance!"

EVA *(trying to pull up* ADITI*)* "Ma, garba dance!"

ADITI *(rubbing her stomach)* You dance.

EVA Relaxed enough for the interview now?

ADITI *nods.* **EVA** *dances.*

ADITI Ewah, I be pay yes?

EVA *(stops dancing)* Yes.

ADITI No stop ban, no stop pay?

EVA We did the transfer in time. Deliver twins and you'll be paid – in full.

ADITI First time I here, many lady. Now many lady go home. Empty hand.

EVA They didn't get pregnant before the ban. You did.

ADITI Other lady work here two, three time. These lady say me do this 'gain. No stop ban, how I work 'gain?

EVA A secret – if the ban continues, Madamji could open clinics in other countries...

ADITI Amrika?

EVA Maybe.

ADITI Then I go.

EVA It won't be that easy.

ADITI You get passport me.

EVA I wouldn't know how.

ADITI You no help?

EVA Why worry about this now? Get through this pregnancy first.

ADITI Many lady here, say parent promise much before go. "We call you from UK, Amrika, Canada, you hear baby talk". Never hear gain. Some parent give wrong number. No number.

EVA *(taking* **ADITI***'s hand)* Not with us.

ADITI *doubles over.*

ADITI Hai...

EVA Aditi?

> ADITI *takes deep breaths, her head bent, holding her stomach.*

What's wrong?

> EVA *holds* ADITI.

The babies?

> ADITI *nods.*

I'm calling Dr. Gupta –

ADITI *(smiling)* Dance.

EVA Dance?

ADITI Ho...

EVA You feel them?

> ADITI *closes her eyes, feeling her stomach with both hands.*

What do you feel?

ADITI *(smiling)* Garba dance...

EVA Garba?

> EVA*'s hand hovers over* ADITI*'s stomach.*

Can I...?

ADITI Ohhh...

EVA Can I...?

ADITI Oof!

EVA Can I feel?

Gently moving away **ADITI**'s *hands,* **EVA** *places her hands on* **ADITI**'s *stomach.* **ADITI** *opens her eyes, guiding* **EVA**'s *hands around her stomach.*

(Moving her hands) No...

ADITI Here.

EVA No... I... I...

ADITI Ohhh...

EVA ...Can't...can't... I...

ADITI Oof!

EVA I...can't feel...my babies...

EVA *moves her hands away.* **ADITI** *closes her eyes, holds her stomach, lost in the touch.* **EVA** *watches, toying with the kurta. Long pause.* **ADITI** *opens her eyes.*

ADITI Boy.

EVA We don't know that yet.

ADITI Kick, punch.

EVA Girls kick and punch too.

ADITI Bhagwan give boy.

EVA You can't know that yet.

ADITI *lies down, feeling her stomach.*

ADITI Manesh want boy. Two time.

EVA I want one boy, one girl.

ADITI No give Manesh boy.

EVA's *phone rings.* **ADITI** *closes her eyes, stroking her stomach.* **EVA** *picks up her phone and checks the screen.*

EVA Shit.

EVA *switches off the phone and puts it away. She unknots her chunni and paces.* ADITI *rises.*

ADITI Husband?

EVA My Masterji, like your Masterji at the dairy farm. I have to work too, to pay for you, for my garba dancing babies –

ADITI But Ewah rich.

EVA Ewah not rich.

ADITI Ewah gori gori Maharani. Too much nice dress, live big UK palace –

EVA I'll be living in a tent if I don't find a paying client quickly.

ADITI *begins sewing the kurta.*

ADITI Ewah, where husband?

EVA *(stops pacing)* My husband?

ADITI Haan, you husband. Where he is?

EVA Not here. Can't be here. Busy with business far from here.

ADITI He no lubb you?

EVA Always.

ADITI You no miss husband?

EVA Always.

ADITI *(stops sewing)* Me miss husband all time.

EVA I know.

ADITI Husband no miss you, miss twin?

EVA If he could be here, he would be here.

ADITI No like India?

EVA Tom loved – loves – India. After we married, he took me to the Taj Mahal –

ADITI Manesh promise me Taj. No time, no rupee, work work. No go now.

EVA Take your girls, after my babies *(strokes* **ADITI***'s stomach)* are born.

ADITI *(stroking her stomach)* Girls miss too much him. Now, I no there also.

EVA He was a fruit and vegetable seller?

ADITI Day, night, push laari.

EVA Like a fruit cart?

ADITI Wood laari. Make own hand.

EVA Tom ran a restaurant. Like a big "dhaba".

ADITI Ewah and Ewah husband rich.

EVA No. We had to sell it, to have a baby.

ADITI Manesh leave nothing us. Only broke wood. *(Pause)* I run so fast. Big car one side. Manesh other. Hold him. Blood wash milk. One peoples help him. Other peoples get rich. Fight like kutha dogs, steal fruit. Rich man fall out car. Too much drink. He look Manesh, look me, get in car. Drive. Life cheap.

EVA *(holding* **ADITI***'s hand)* I didn't know – I'm so sorry –

ADITI Ewah, no ever let go husband. Life lone, too hard.

EVA Yes.

ADITI Bhagwan bless you all thing. You has all thing.

EVA I don't –

ADITI Lot money, good husband, two baby –

EVA No –

ADITI I pray my husband be live, same you husband –

EVA No Aditi –

ADITI Care two baby, when you no there –

EVA   No he won't –

ADITI   – hold baby, laugh baby, grow baby –

EVA   No he won't because he's dead.

ADITI   Haan?

EVA   My husband died. Cancer.

ADITI   You husband?

EVA   About three years ago.

ADITI   Die?

EVA   I've been trying to have our baby ever since.

ADITI   Three year for baby in UK?

EVA   Sort of.

ADITI   India, only nine month.

EVA   That's why I'm here.

Pause.

ADITI   Ewah, how you make baby with dead husband?

EVA   I only needed my husband's...seed.

ADITI   Seed?

EVA   To join with my egg.

ADITI   Haan?

EVA   Madamji didn't explain how all this is done?

ADITI   She say my tum tum garba pot for you. Fire there *(pointing at the lit pot)*, baby here *(patting her stomach)*.

EVA   We joined my husband's seed with my egg. Put them inside you.

ADITI   But he dead...

EVA   He died but his seed was still alive.

ADITI   Haan?

EVA A miracle. Bhagwan's work. My husband lives through his seed. In you. In the babies. Waiting to be born again –

ADITI *(hyperventilating)* Dead man – in me?

EVA Oh no, there's no dead man in you –

> ADITI *rubs the make-up from her face.*

– only my two babies.

> ADITI *tears the flowers from her hair and hurls them away.*

Tom died far away, in the UK.

> ADITI *pushes* EVA *away.*

ADITI Dead gora, dead seed –?

EVA Nothing dead / in you.

ADITI Dead / dead?

EVA My babies moved inside you. Not my dead husband, not your dead husband, no dead husband –

ADITI *(stops)* Manesh?

EVA Let me show you.

> EVA *rushes to her bag and pulls out a scan.*

See – my scan. *(Pointing)* One, two babies. Babies. See the tiny head, body, arms, legs, little hands waving –

> ADITI *pushes the scan away in horror. She stuffs the photo and kurta into her plastic bag.*

What are you doing?

> ADITI *tries to move past* EVA, *who blocks* ADITI.

ADITI I...go.

EVA Where?

ADITI Daughters.

EVA You can't. Your mother-in-law doesn't want you to visit them.

ADITI I no care.

EVA She'll get angry with you –

ADITI I give money her. Madamji make account, I give money her –

EVA No good for you, the twins, the girls, not anyone –

ADITI I go –

EVA You're carrying the twins, need rest –

>ADITI *tries to move past* EVA *again.* EVA *blocks her.*

ADITI I get bus.

EVA You can't just leave –

>ADITI *holds back her tears.*

– and get on a bus.

>EVA *prises the plastic bag from* ADITI.

You'll be back with your daughters before you know –

>ADITI *cries.*

– like you were never away.

ADITI *(hitting her stomach)* What you do?

>EVA *grabs* ADITI'*s arms, as* ADITI *tries to pull away.*

(Crying) What you do?... What you do?

EVA Aditi, when my husband was dying, there was a nurse. She made him laugh when I couldn't smile, held his hands when mine trembled, wiped his tears when I couldn't see through mine. You – you look so much like her. When I saw your photo, it had to be you. She was a gift from God.

From Bhagwan. Like you're mine. You say I have everything.
I don't. You do. You had two beautiful children with your
husband. My husband died before we could have children of
our own. You have everything. You're giving me everything.
(Pause) Life.

Pause. **ADITI** *composes herself.*

ADITI I see Rajni, Rekha, today.

EVA You need to stay here –

ADITI Only one day.

EVA Madamji won't agree.

ADITI No tell her.

EVA We'd have to.

ADITI Take me my girls.

EVA You'll be stuck in a car for hours.

ADITI Car ok when drive me rally, interview –?

EVA This would be a much longer journey.

ADITI Take me them now.

EVA Soon.

ADITI This important. Please.

EVA I promise.

> **ADITI** *strokes her stomach and sings a Gujarati lullaby
> to her bump.* **EVA** *watches. As darkness descends, two
> foetuses from a 20-week ultrasound, dance on the dorm
> walls to the lullaby. The ultrasound blends into footage
> of* **ADITI**, **DR. GUPTA** *and* **EVA** *in a TV studio, as* **ADITI***'s
> lullaby fades out.*

Scene Three

Empty clinic wing.

Scattered chairs in an empty pink room. Bottles and empty glasses stand on one of the chairs. **DR. GUPTA** *and* **EVA** *enter, in an excited state.* **ADITI** *follows.* **EVA** *is dressed in a smart linen suit,* **DR. GUPTA** *and* **ADITI** *in colourful saris and chappals.* **EVA** *pulls out a chair for* **ADITI**, *who sits, her big baby bump growing.*

DR. GUPTA "Ban the ban?"

EVA I couldn't have phrased it better!

DR. GUPTA *That* should be our new slogan.

EVA *(to* **ADITI***)* What made you think of it?

ADITI I answer the man's every question, same Madamji and you teach me.

EVA *(to* **DR. GUPTA***)* So it was you?

DR. GUPTA All hers.

EVA *(to* **ADITI***)* "Ban the ban", "My body, my choice" – my Masterji should give you a job.

ADITI Promise?

DR. GUPTA *(to* **EVA***)* You'll have to fight Thakkar for her. He says she's been a real asset to his campaign.

ADITI Promise Ewah?

EVA The face of our campaign was the star of the show!

DR. GUPTA Thirty minutes on prime time TV? Everyone wants to talk to us now!

EVA *(to* **DR. GUPTA***)* Oh, I loved it when you said, "Why deny –'

EVA and **DR. GUPTA** '– people the right to be parents just because they're dead?'

ADITI *shifts uncomfortably in her chair, getting up and pacing.*

DR. GUPTA If the science exists to benefit all parties, why not use it? Society will catch up.

EVA Why aren't you standing for election?

DR. GUPTA Thakkar asks me too. Champions me as a model feminist entrepreneur –

ADITI *paces around, controlling her breathing.*

EVA – and a TV natural!

DR. GUPTA Let's toast our formidable team. *(Picking up a bottle of wine. To* EVA*)* Indian wine? We've been making wine since the fourth century BC.

DR. GUPTA *pours a couple of glasses.*

EVA We won't get arrested?

DR. GUPTA In this nanny state? Who knows? They'll ignore daily rapes and violence against girls and women but ban everything "bad" – alcohol, surrogacy for foreigners, gays, single people...

DR. GUPTA *pours a small bottle of Coca-Cola into a glass, handing it to* ADITI.

Coca-Cola, the champagne of the masses, for you!

ADITI Thank you Madamji.

DR. GUPTA *and* EVA *raise their glasses.* ADITI *awkwardly follows.*

DR. GUPTA To sisterhood!

EVA Sisterhood.

ADITI "Sister"...like "Didi"?

DR. GUPTA Haan – and "hood".

ADITI *(raising her glass)* "Didi-hood".

ALL "Didi-hood".

> **EVA** *and* **DR. GUPTA** *laugh. They all clink and drink.*

DR. GUPTA *(to* **EVA***)* To mark our Didihood, I have a gift for you.

> **DR. GUPTA** *picks up a red and yellow thread from the table.*

Raksha – a sacred thread to protect you and your unborn twins.

EVA You're spoiling me.

> **DR. GUPTA** *ties the thread around* **EVA***'s right wrist.*

DR. GUPTA You should drink milk before you tie but boozeleg wine works just as well.

EVA I feel so blessed.

DR. GUPTA Remember, it's bad luck to break the thread.

EVA I won't let it break.

ADITI *(rubbing her stomach)* Madamji, hot tum tum sun –

> **EVA***'s phone rings.*

Sick feel.

DR. GUPTA *(to* **EVA***)* I'll take her. *(Ushering out* **ADITI***)* Challo.

EVA *(answering her phone)* Hi Mike, how are you?... Yes all ok... No not a problem to speak... No it's not interfering... I know it's been a rough few years and I appreciate all your support... What about everything we've done together? Business I've created?... I can't afford... Please if you give me a few more weeks I will be back...

> **DR. GUPTA** *returns, moving to one side.*

(On the phone) I can't afford, I can't afford. Ok right. Thanks Mike. *(Hangs up)*

DR. GUPTA *(to* EVA*)* All ok?

EVA *(gulping her wine)* Fine thanks. Is Aditi ok?

DR. GUPTA Rising and falling like the Ganges... So, how is our clinic brand work going?

EVA I've had some other work I needed to do.

DR. GUPTA With all this publicity, we should move quickly.

EVA Dr. Gupta...circumstances have slightly changed.

DR. GUPTA How?

EVA I – I can no longer afford to work pro-bono.

DR. GUPTA Why?

> EVA *swigs a gulp of wine.*

EVA I – I just got the sack.

DR. GUPTA I'm sorry.

EVA Maybe we could agree a fee.

DR. GUPTA I can't afford to pay you.

EVA I can't afford to work for free.

DR. GUPTA You made a deal.

EVA That I have to rescind.

DR. GUPTA You rescinded your bills too? I'm still waiting for you to settle those.

EVA I'm sorry it's taking so long. I've had to settle other bills – lawyers' fees, court fees, endless debts just to be here. Borrowed from my mother, friends, I can't ask them again –

DR. GUPTA You still haven't paid your transfer bill, second and third installments, increased costs for twins, plus extras. I've also put my money into the campaign, with zero contribution from you –

EVA If you hadn't charged so much for the transfer –

DR. GUPTA You asked me to charge a fair price, I did –

EVA More than quadruple the original cost? Plus numerous hidden costs, sudden extras, I might have paid earlier.

DR. GUPTA This isn't a haggling bazaar.

EVA I'm bankrupt! Ok?

> *Pause.*

DR. GUPTA Then Eva, why are you here?

> *Pause.* ADITI *comes back in, wiping her mouth, rubbing her stomach. She tries making eye contact with* EVA, *who turns away.*

ADITI Baby burn. Baby make fire. Hava blow.

DR. GUPTA You want to tell her or should I?

EVA Tell her what?

DR. GUPTA She hasn't been paid. Because you failed to make your payments.

EVA You didn't pay her from clinic funds?

DR. GUPTA The ban has almost wiped out my clinic funds. Aditi's account is now bound up with yours.

ADITI *(to* DR. GUPTA *in Gujarati)* What you say Madamji?

DR. GUPTA *(to* ADITI*)* Eva hasn't paid her bills, so we had to delay paying you –

ADITI *(to* DR. GUPTA *in Gujarati)* Manesh Ma no get money?

EVA *(to* DR. GUPTA*)* You really couldn't have paid her?

ADITI *(to* EVA*)* You no pay me more money?

EVA *(to* DR. GUPTA*)* It isn't fair she loses out.

DR. GUPTA *(to* EVA*)* Then pay your bills.

ADITI *(to* EVA*)* Why you no pay?

EVA Aditi, I lost my job.

ADITI You ok Ewah. You got lot money.

EVA I don't.

ADITI Where rest / my money?

EVA We'll work something out.

ADITI This why no take me see daughter?

DR. GUPTA *(to* EVA*)* You said you would take her?

ADITI They no eat. I no there, money no there –

EVA You'll get all your money, every last rupee.

ADITI Give me now.

EVA I'm giving you everything I can.

ADITI Give me.

EVA I've nothing more to give you right now.

ADITI Pay me cheap. Treat me cheap. I fill stomach with babies
to fill with food!

ADITI *smashes the bottle of wine on the floor.*

DR. GUPTA Aditi!

ADITI Still my daughters no eat!

DR. GUPTA *scrambles around picking up glass fragments
from the floor.*

EVA I promise you'll be paid all the money you're owed.

ADITI No enough –

EVA Once it's paid, it will be more than enough –

ADITI No enough. Family no talk me. Say I do dirty with other
man. Cause I dirty womans who sell body, then sell my
babies –

EVA They're not your babies.

ADITI *starts hitting her stomach.* EVA *and* DR. GUPTA *rush to intervene.*

DR. GUPTA Stop / Aditi!

EVA Stop!

ADITI *tries to pound her stomach.* EVA *tries grabbing* ADITI's *hands.*

Please stop! Stop!

DR. GUPTA Bhagwan blessed you with these babies!

EVA *and* DR. GUPTA *try to restrain* ADITI.

Don't anger Bhagwan now!

ADITI *stops and breathes heavily, shaking up* EVA.

ADITI Baby die in village all time.

DR. GUPTA Aditi please –

ADITI I see it all. *(In Gujarati)* I carry twin many month. *(In English)* I no leave here empty hand.

DR. GUPTA You will leave empty-handed if you harm those babies.

ADITI *(in Gujarati)* What you put in here? *(In English)* Dead man seed.

DR. GUPTA We don't explain details to the surrogate. You're paid to carry and deliver.

ADITI My body, my choice?

DR. GUPTA Haan.

ADITI *(to* EVA*)* Pay me baby.

EVA What? /

DR. GUPTA Aditi –

ADITI Pay me baby. There two. One, two.

EVA Those are *my* babies.

ADITI No pay, my baby.

EVA I will pay.

ADITI I want –

EVA I said I'll pay.

ADITI – boy.

EVA Those are *my* babies.

DR. GUPTA *(to* **ADITI***)* We have a contract.

ADITI *(to* **DR. GUPTA***)* Contract nothing me. Your word nothing me. Pay me baby.

DR. GUPTA You can't demand –

ADITI Campaign big lie. Baby big lie. Should never have born.

EVA *(to* **ADITI***)* How can you say that?

ADITI *(to* **DR. GUPTA***)* I tell all.

DR. GUPTA We did the transfer in time.

ADITI Late.

DR. GUPTA In time.

ADITI All peoples know this face, campaign face, peoples listen me – I no lie. This face tell all peoples Madamji lie me.

DR. GUPTA Aditi, we haven't lied.

ADITI No tell me dead man seed, no tell me no pay, no tell me daughter starve, no tell what put in me –

DR. GUPTA I have to protect all my surrogates and babies –

ADITI All other lady, we talk also –

DR. GUPTA The surrogates?

ADITI We finish you, finish clinic, finish Thakkar.

　　ADITI *breathes heavily.* **DR. GUPTA** *is silent.*

Baby.

Pause.

DR. GUPTA *(turning to* EVA*)* If you can't pay –

EVA You're saying... I...?

> EVA *chokes.*

DR. GUPTA You should have paid your way Memsahib, as promised.

> *Pause.* EVA *takes out a wad of rupees from her bag and hurls the notes into the air.*

EVA Here!

> *The notes flutter down, all around.* DR. GUPTA *is motionless.* ADITI *grabs the notes around her as they fall.*

I keep these for the constant beggars!

> ADITI *grabs rupees from the floor, holding fistfuls of notes.* EVA *sobs.* DR. GUPTA *tries taking hold of* ADITI, *who breathes heavily.*

DR. GUPTA Aditi come –

ADITI Manesh in me. This time, I no let go him, no let go –

> ADITI *pushes away* DR. GUPTA.

DR. GUPTA *(to* ADITI *in Gujarati)* Let's go back to the dorm –

ADITI Take money take baby take take take –!

> ADITI *collapses. Lights out. A 3D 28-week scan of two babies swirls on the clinic walls. The two babies float and move, waving limbs. Suddenly, one baby falls still.* DR. GUPTA*'s voice blends in "Throwing off the shackles of socialism, Mother India was getting back her respect, her dignity, especially in Gujarat, a desert land where milk and money now flow. Keep her part of that Shining*

New India, its beating heart, quickening pulse. Not left behind".

Scene Four

The dorm.

Darkness shrouds the dorm. **ADITI** *is asleep. A diya burns in a shrine, beside an empty garba pot. Wearing an Indian suit and chunni,* **EVA** *sits alongside* **ADITI**. **ADITI** *begins to wake.*

ADITI *(groggy)* Stay...

EVA Aditi?

ADITI *(opens her eyes)* Where –?

EVA How are you?

ADITI ...he go?

EVA Who?

ADITI Manesh?

EVA *(teary)* He's not here.

ADITI *(touching her stomach)* With me. Here.

EVA *(teary)* He isn't here.

ADITI "We born, die, born gain... No cry...what no stop."

    EVA *holds back tears.* **ADITI** *rubs her stomach.*

    Heavy.

EVA *(taking* **ADITI**'s *hand)* Aditi –

ADITI Boys sleep. Heavy sleep. No punch, kick today.

EVA Aditi...one of the twins...died.

ADITI No... *(Rubs her stomach)* I feel.

EVA We lost one of the babies.

ADITI Madam say both ok.

EVA We lost one.

ADITI She say me when I wake first.

> EVA *shakes her head.*

No...no lie, no cheat.

EVA I'm not.

ADITI *(welling up)* You lie gain.

EVA How could I?

ADITI I feel...

> EVA *shakes her head.*

They heavy...

EVA I know.

ADITI *(weeps)* Like stone.

EVA Yes.

> EVA *bows her head.*

ADITI *(panicking)* Dead?

> ADITI *rubs her belly manically.*

My baby –

EVA You have to / stay calm.

ADITI – dead –?

EVA *(calming* ADITI*)* Aditi please –

ADITI Dead man dead seed / dead baby in me –

EVA We'll get / through this.

ADITI Take him / out –

EVA You and me / we'll get through this.

ADITI Out! Out!

ADITI *wails.* DR. GUPTA *rushes in.* EVA *moves away from* ADITI. DR. GUPTA *holds* ADITI, *who sobs in* DR. GUPTA's *arms.*

DR. GUPTA *(to* ADITI*)* Chup... Chup...

DR. GUPTA *rocks* ADITI, *calming her.*

(To ADITI*)* Bheta, think about the other baby.

ADITI *(to* DR. GUPTA *in Gujarati)* You didn't tell me...again...

DR. GUPTA *(to* ADITI*)* Your Madamji always has to protect you first –

ADITI *(to* DR. GUPTA *in Gujarati)* ...what happen inside...

DR. GUPTA *(looking at* EVA, *to* ADITI*)* Not till you were stronger.

DR. GUPTA *smoothes* ADITI's *hair, rocking her gently.*

(To ADITI*)* You're blessed Yashoda Ma with her baby Krishna.

ADITI *(to* DR. GUPTA*)* Give my baby to Bhagwan. Take him out. Out.

DR. GUPTA *(to* ADITI*)* If we take out the baby, we'll lose the other baby too.

ADITI *cradles her belly and weeps.* DR. GUPTA *wipes* ADITI's *tears dry.*

(To ADITI*)* No tears. *(Pause)* The baby can hear, feel...

ADITI *(to* DR. GUPTA*)* I know... I know... Manesh hears. Feels.

Long pause. ADITI *wriggles free of* DR. GUPTA, *wipes her face, slips on her chappals and rises.*

Bathroom.

DR. GUPTA *(to* ADITI *in Gujarati)* I'll take you.

ADITI No, I go.

ADITI *shuffles out, cradling her stomach, kicking over the garba pot as she goes.*

DR. GUPTA *(approaching* EVA*)* Why tell her?

EVA I had to.

DR. GUPTA For you or for her?

EVA For her.

DR. GUPTA Leave my clinic. Come back for your caesarian. You already know the day and time. Be grateful I'll even let you do that.

EVA I'm staying.

DR. GUPTA Get out.

EVA I'm not leaving till my baby is born.

DR. GUPTA Since you arrived, you've caused problems.

EVA I've been protecting my babies –

DR. GUPTA If you had just paid up, left me to it –

EVA – protecting my babies from you.

DR. GUPTA Excuse me?

EVA Did you kill my baby?

DR. GUPTA What? Your baby died from severe discordant foetal growth – the bigger twin receiving too much blood flow, the smaller twin too little –

EVA I want a second opinion.

DR. GUPTA You're not taking my surrogate out of my clinic. Not in her state.

EVA Because it isn't that is it? *You* killed my baby.

DR. GUPTA What I did was make a mistake. Doing the transfer, letting you into my dorm, making up your own rules, making a mess, leaving others to clean up –

EVA Is this your transaction?

DR. GUPTA My clinic, my rules.

EVA That you've bent and broken to serve and profit yourself –

DR. GUPTA Only me?

EVA – while you raised and milked your herd of cattle? I understand.

DR. GUPTA You understand? Don some traditional dress, bindis, bangles, eat curry, do yoga – and you understand? You'll never understand us the way we had to understand you. When things are taken from you, you learn to take back. You got enough for free. Now it's your time to pay.

EVA You're sick.

DR. GUPTA Business. No different to buying a pair of trainers.

EVA I lost my baby.

DR. GUPTA You're still getting more than you've paid for.

EVA You did something.

DR. GUPTA You've been here too long. Indian heat.

EVA Life and death, it's easy for you isn't it?

DR. GUPTA If it's so easy, be careful Eva.

EVA Don't you dare threaten me. *(Pause)* I'll call the police.

DR. GUPTA *(holding out her phone)* Call them.

EVA I'll make sure you won't have a clinic left to run –

DR. GUPTA And you won't leave India as a mother.

> DR. GUPTA's *phone rings.*

> She has a claim.

EVA You –

> DR. GUPTA *answers her phone.*

DR. GUPTA Haan? I'll be down right away. *(Hangs up)* Aditi's
gone.

*A 3D 28-week scan of two babies, one moving, one still,
swirl on the clinic walls.* **ADITI** *voices a final election
appeal "Vote for a Better India – a Brave New India".*

Blackout.

TRIMESTER THREE

Scene One

Diwali.

Village shack.

Election Night. Gujarati music pounds and fireworks explode outside, lighting up the one-room shack in flashes. A smoky haze fills the space. A chair blocks the door. A Hindi alphabet chart and children's drawings are pinned to the burnt sienna walls. Two baby kurtas hang on a line, strung across the room. A diya burns in a shrine in a corner. A colourful garba pot holds a knife. On a floor messy with blood and bodily fluids, two bricks have been placed feet apart. A dead white baby lies in a plastic bucket, an umbilical cord wound round the baby's neck. Lying exhausted, in a red sari pulled up to her thighs, **ADITI** *holds a bloodied white baby close. She wipes the blood and fluids from the baby's face and body with a wet cloth. The wooden door bangs.* **ADITI** *and* **DR. GUPTA** *speak in Gujarati. (The first two lines can be delivered in Gujarati, the rest in English).*

DR. GUPTA *(offstage)* Aditi? Aditi?

> **DR. GUPTA** *bangs on the door.* **ADITI** *reaches for the knife, keeping it close.*

(Offstage) Open the door! *(Banging on the door)* Aditi!

> **DR. GUPTA** *pushes the door forcefully until it bursts open. In a crumpled sari and chappals, she carries a medical case in her hand.*

(Looking around) Oh God.

> **DR. GUPTA** *closes the door and moves towards* **ADITI**.

Is the baby alright?

ADITI *holds the knife towards* DR. GUPTA.

You?

DR. GUPTA *stops and notices the dead baby in the bucket.*

The dead one?

ADITI *(nods towards the baby, smiling)* A girl. *(Holds the baby in her arms close)* A boy. Manesh.

DR. GUPTA *takes out a scalpel from her medical case and moves closer.*

DR. GUPTA I need to check the cord.

ADITI *(holding out the knife)* Stay back.

DR. GUPTA Aditi, please listen to me.

ADITI Stay back!

ADITI *holds the baby close.*

DR. GUPTA He looks pale.

ADITI *(admiring him)* He's beautiful.

DR. GUPTA He's premature –

ADITI *(to the baby)* We're fine, aren't we?

DR. GUPTA – needs urgent medical help.

ADITI We're home.

DR. GUPTA If you stay here, you're both in danger.

ADITI Your clinic is safe?

The baby cries. ADITI *feeds the baby from her breast.*

DR. GUPTA Don't breast-feed him.

ADITI He's hungry.

DR. GUPTA It's not in your contract.

ADITI The contract, all for her?

DR. GUPTA Stop breast-feeding him.

ADITI You want him to starve too?

DR. GUPTA He's not yours.

ADITI More mine than hers.

DR. GUPTA You could have killed him. You could still kill him.

ADITI I birthed him.

DR. GUPTA You're just a vessel.

ADITI I fed him. Grew him. My blood. My milk.

DR. GUPTA A garba pot.

ADITI Liar.

DR. GUPTA "The ovum, not the womb, makes the mother". Eva owns him. You're stealing from her.

　　ADITI *laughs.*

　　You signed a contract.

ADITI You broke the law.

DR. GUPTA Honour it.

ADITI Honour?

　　Pause.

　　He's staying here, with me. Honest life.

DR. GUPTA A hard life.

ADITI Less hard for a boy. *(Points to the dead baby)* Better she's dead.

DR. GUPTA If you love him, you won't keep him.

ADITI He's made in India.

DR. GUPTA He's made to order. She's paying.

ADITI I'm his mother. A woman too.

Pause.

DR. GUPTA Aditi, be a Mother India. Sacrifice yourself, serve your nation. All your children. *(Holds out her hands)* Give him to me.

ADITI He needs me.

DR. GUPTA Your daughters need you. He needs his life out there.

ADITI We don't want anything more from you. *(Holding the baby close)* We have everything we need.

DR. GUPTA There isn't a court in India that will let you keep him.

ADITI Even after I tell the whole world everything you did?

DR. GUPTA Even then.

ADITI I might lose everything – but you will too.

Pause. DR. GUPTA *swoops forward, knocks the knife from* ADITI's *hand and cuts the cord with the scalpel, pulling the crying baby from* ADITI. ADITI *resists, before capitulating and sobbing.* DR. GUPTA *checks the baby and then, a limp* ADITI. DR. GUPTA *takes a cheque from inside her case, holding it out for* ADITI.

DR. GUPTA All I owe, plus double for the twins – and a bonus. More work when you need. A future.

ADITI *does not take the cheque.* DR. GUPTA *pushes it into* ADITI's *hand.*

Buy brand new lives for you and your daughters.

ADITI *tries to rip up the cheque but cannot.* DR. GUPTA *packs up her case and walks to the door. She turns back.*

Thakkar lost.

ADITI New India, get out of my house.

*Lit up by exploding fireworks and to the sounds of a
gathering crowd outside,* **DR. GUPTA** *opens the door
and walks out, holding the crying baby in her arms.*
ADITI *slowly picks up the cheque and places it inside
the garba pot. She sits up on the blood-soaked floor with
difficulty and picks up the dead baby girl from the
bucket, unwinding the umbilical cord from her neck.*
ADITI *holds the dead baby close, crying and gently
rocking her, singing her a Gujarati lullaby.*

EPILOGUE

Lajja Gauri Fertility Clinic.

Meeting room.

Street sounds cascade into the room. Political chants drown out honking cars, rickshaws and jangling cowbells. Firecrackers explode. A blood red sunset spills through the closed iron-barred window. Patches of peeling paint jostle with curling posters of the Virgin Mary with baby Jesus, Krishna and Goddess Lajja Gauri. Packed and half-packed boxes are scattered all over. The ceiling fan is broken. **EVA** *looks dishevelled in a light sweater and jeans, her hair unkempt. Pacing, she fidgets with her phone and swigs from an empty bottle of water. A baby cries outside the room.* **EVA** *moves towards the crying.* **DR. GUPTA** *enters in her crumpled, soiled sari.*

EVA Where is he?

DR. GUPTA Next door, with a nurse, in the Collection Room.

EVA That's him?

DR. GUPTA Powerful set of lungs.

EVA Can I have him now?

DR. GUPTA Not yet.

EVA Not yet?

DR. GUPTA Your bill.

EVA After everything?

DR. GUPTA It remains unpaid.

EVA He could have died.

DR. GUPTA He didn't.

EVA Haven't I paid enough?

DR. GUPTA I'm as shaken as you are –

EVA No you're not.

DR. GUPTA Do you hear him?

> *Pause.* EVA *sits, exhausted, on a chair. She pulls out her chequebook.*

EVA How much do I owe?

> DR. GUPTA *sits opposite* EVA. *Long pause.*

DR. GUPTA Just take him. Let's leave everything else here.

> *Pause.* EVA *puts away her chequebook and stands.*

EVA Thank you.

DR. GUPTA *(standing)* The last foreign baby in my clinic.

EVA We did it –

DR. GUPTA We didn't stop the ban.

EVA If you need me and the baby for any –

DR. GUPTA No.

EVA *(looking around)* You're packing?

DR. GUPTA Downsizing for now. Shifting abroad. Where we can, while we can.

EVA Lajja Gauri lives on.

DR. GUPTA Only just. Thakkar and a few of his friends invested.

EVA Congratulations.

DR. GUPTA I'll still fight for our women. All women.

EVA You're the woman for that.

> EVA *holds out her hand for* DR. GUPTA.

DR. GUPTA You're not wearing the thread.

EVA It broke.

They shake hands.

DR. GUPTA He's in the Collection Room. Nurse will take you.

EVA collects her bag and exits. **DR. GUPTA** *packs some boxes, takes down and rolls up the posters. Moments later,* **EVA** *returns, holding the baby.*

EVA Dr. Gupta?

EVA carries the baby towards **DR. GUPTA**.

This is... Tom.

DR. GUPTA Namaste Tom. Welcome to our world.

******

A blood-red light fills the empty interior. **DR. GUPTA** *stands alone, dressed in a white medical coat over a sari and heels.* **ADITI** *enters, wearing a mud-stained white sari and chappals.*

ADITI Madamji, I need to go again.

Lights out.

PROPERTY LIST

The action mostly takes place inside the Lajja Gauri Fertility
Clinic in Gujarat, India. For the 2017 world premier production,
Lydia Denno's fabric medical screens created a womb-like set.
These screens established the clinic and then evolved to allow
the actors to use them, for example as doors for entrances/exits,
to double as medical and modesty screens, as vertical medical/
dorm beds – even concealing hooks to hang props.

Many props written in this script (to create specific worlds)
were discarded for the production. Minimal props (including
just two plastic chairs) were used to focus the women's lives,
bodies and emotions, declutter the space and allow the action
to flow. Many of these discarded props are listed as optional.

Depending on the creative vision of director and designer,
in a play in which staging is encouraged to be abstract and
impressionistic, the following list is intended to be suggestive
and selective rather than too prescriptive. Subsequent
productions and creative teams are free to find their own design
concepts and solutions.

Trimester 1

White mother and white baby posters (p1) optional
Religious posters – Virgin Mary and baby Jesus, Krishna,
Goddess Lajja Gauri (p1) optional
Plastic chairs (p1)
Eva's travel case (p1) optional
Eva's bag (p1)
Eva's file (p1/with sheets p5)
Dr. Gupta's medical coat (p1)
Dr. Gupta's phone (p1)
Dr. Gupta's marigolds for Eva (p1)
Eva's newspaper (p2)
Eva's bottled water (p7)
Aditi's plastic bag (p7)
Eva's phone (p12)

Eva's medical gown (p15)
Dr. Gupta's medical file (p15)
Eva's IV (p15) optional
Dr. Gupta's latex gloves and box (p16)
Eva's IV line (p19) optional
Eva's henna tattoo (p19) optional
Eva's medical hairnet (p20)
Dr. Gupta's surgical mask (p20)

Aditi's medical gown and hairnet (as Eva's before) (p22) optional
Aditi's crumpled photo (p27)

Trimester 2

"Vote Thakkar" posters (p30) optional
Two glasses of Lassi (p30)
Lotus pendant necklace (p31)

Eva and Aditi's jasmine flowers (p38) optional
Colourful garba pot (p38)
Baby kurta top (p38) optional
Sewing needle for baby kurta top (p42) optional
Baby scan (p45)

Wine bottle, Coca-Cola bottle and three glasses (p48)
Red and yellow raksha thread (p50)
Eva's wad of rupee notes (p56)

Indian shrine (lit by a diya) (p58) optional

Trimester 3

Hindi alphabet chart (p64) optional
Children's drawings (p64) optional
Baby kurta 2 (p64) optional
Aditi's knife (p64)
Two bricks (p64) optional
Plastic bucket (p64)
Wet cloth (p64) optional
Dr. Gupta's medical case (p64)

Dr. Gupta's scalpel (p65) optional
A cheque (p67)

Epilogue

Cardboard boxes (p69) optional
Eva's chequebook (p70)

SOUND EFFECTS

The offstage sounds create the bigger Indian world outside the clinic. The ringing telephone and Eva's work phone calls press on this insular world, a technological connection to the UK and the West. In keeping with the slightly out-of-time quality of the play, Eva's first two routine work calls take place slightly out of the scenes, out of time, to suggest they happen more frequently, before those particular scenes properly begin.

The transitions are coloured by music, projections and voiceovers, creating the individual and collective consciousness of the characters. Arun Ghosh's soundscape threaded Indian influenced music through other worlds of the play – heartbeats, ringtones, voices, radio and TV soundbites and excerpts of political speeches. Depending on technical resources and limitations, these transitions are not essential and can be edited down and selectively represented so there is a suggested visual/aural continuity between scenes.

In the production, the offstage male character of Thakkar was given voiceovers (most notably at the top of Trimester 1 Scene 3) but other voiceovers and speech excerpts can also be kept solely between the three characters.

OFFSTAGE SOUND EFFECTS

Trimester 1

Political chants (p1)
Street sounds (honking cars, rickshaws, cowbells, street vendors) (p1)
Ceiling fan (p1) optional
Transition: music/syringe projection/speech excerpt (p13/14)

Eva's loud ringing phone (p15)
(Continued through part of the scene)

Transition: music/chants/Puja and petri dish IVF projections (p21)

Voice on a background radio (p22)

Transition: music/embryo transfer projection/chants into heartbeats/ first ultrasound projection (p29)

Trimester 2

Street sounds, crackling oil, Bollywood music (p30)
Eva's ringing phone (p30)

Transition: music/media montage/twin baby ultrasound projection/Dr. Gupta speech excerpt (p36/37)

Gujarati dance music (p38)
Eva's ringing phone (p41)

Transition: Aditi lullaby/twin baby ultrasound projection/TV footage of Aditi, Dr. Gupta and Eva (p47)

Eva's ringing phone (p50)

Transition: music/twin baby ultrasound projection/Dr. Gupta voiceover (p56/57)

Dr. Gupta's ringing phone (p62)

Transition: music/twin baby ultrasound projection/Aditi voiceover (p63)

Trimester 3

Gujarati music/Diwali and election fireworks (p64) optional
Banging door (p64) optional
Crying baby (p65)

Crowd sounds/fireworks (p68) optional

Transition: Aditi lullaby (p68)

Epilogue

Street sounds/chants/firecrackers (p69) optional
Crying baby (p69)

LIGHTING

Set in a womb-like Indian space, the lighting gradually colours
from a stark bright white clinical light/Indian spring sunlight at
the beginning of the play to a blood red light/autumnal Indian
sunset light by the end, slowly bleeding yellow, pink, brown and
red tones into the set.

Trimester 1

Lights up: interior bright white sunlight (p1)
Lights down (p13)

Lights up: interior (sun)light (p15)
Lights down (p21)

Lights up: interior (sun)light (p22)
Lights down (p29)

Trimester 2

Lights up: interior/exterior hazy sunlight (p30)
Lights down (p36)

Lights up: interior pinkish sunlight (p38)
Lights down (p47)

Lights up: interior pink light (p48)
Lights down (p56)

Lights up: interior brown tinged diya (candle) light in darkness (p58)
Lights down (p63)

Trimester 3

Lights up: interior red tinged diya light/firework flashes (optional) (p64)
Lights down (p68)

Epilogue

Lights up: interior blood red sunset light (p69)
Lights down (p71)

Lights up: interior blood red sunset light (p71)
Lights down (p71)

Glossary

Arrey bhai! Itna mahange kyon? Oh brother! Why is it so expensive?
Bazaar Market
Bhaito Sit
Bhagwan God
Bharat Mata Ki Jai Victory to Mother India
Bindi a decorative mark worn in the middle of the forehead by Indian women, especially Hindus
Chappals Sandals
Chunni a length of material worn across the torso (in various ways) but typically worn with a shalwar kameez
Dena tai toh deh If you're going to give it, then give it
Dhaba a roadside food stall
Garba a form of dance originating from Gujarat, India. The name is derived from the Sanskrit term for womb (Garbha) and is a celebration of the ability to create new life.
Garba pot a clay pot traditionally placed at the centre of the Garba dancing circle
Gota popular snack in Gujarat made of fried batter
Gori a white woman
Krishna Hindu deity. Krishna is the "bhagavan-svayam": the ultimate, highest and original manifestation of God
Kurta a long, loosely fitted collarless shirt worn by people from South Asia, usually with a shalwar, churidars, or pyjama
Kutha a dog
Lajja Gauri goddess associated with abundance and fertility
Laari a barrow on which people sell goods by the roadside or in markets
Lassi a sweet or savoury Indian drink made from a yogurt or buttermilk base with water
Madamji Madam
Mehndi decorative designs on the body, using a paste made from powdered dry leaves of a henna plant

Pallu loose end of a sari

Rupee the currency of India, Pakistan, Sri Lanka, Nepal, Mauritius and the Seychelles

Sadhu A holy man, sage or ascetic

Sari draped dress created from a single piece of fabric wrapped around a woman's body a variety of ways

Shalwar kameez traditional garment that resembles a tunic or long shirt and worn primarily by women

Yashoda Ma foster mother to Krishna. Known as a devoted and selfless mother

ABOUT THE AUTHOR

Satinder Kaur Chohan is from Southall, West London and completed her BA in English Language and Literature at King's College London and her MA at Yale University in the US. A journalist and documentary researcher/assistant producer turned playwright, her plays include *Zameen* (Kali Theatre national tour 2008), *KabaddiKabaddiKabaddi* (Pursued By A Bear national tour 2012), *1984* (Vibrant Festival 2014 Finborough Theatre) and *Lotus Beauty*, a 2016 Sultan Padamsee Award for Playwriting Runner-Up. Satinder received OffWestEnd.com's 2013 Adopt A Playwright Award to develop *Made in India*. As Writer-in-Residence at the Centre for Family Research (University of Cambridge), she wrote *Half of Me*, first performed by Generation Arts in Summer 2016 (Lyric Hammersmith). *Half of Me* accompanies *Made in India* at select venues on tour.

Other plays by SATINDER KAUR CHOHAN published and licensed by Concord Theatricals

Half of Me

Zameen